YOU KNOW YOU'RE A VIDEO GAME ADDICT IF...

BY RYAN G. VAN CLEAVE

RUNNING PRESS
PHILADELPHIA · LONDON

Books published by Running Press are available at special discounts for bulk purchases in the United States by corporations, institutions, and other organizations. For more information, please contact the Special Markets Department at the Perseus Books Group, 2300 Chestnut Street, Suite 200, Philadelphia, PA 19103, or call (800) 810-4145, ext. 5000, or e-mail special.markets@perseusbooks.com.

ISBN 978-0-7624-4377-2

Library of Congress Control Number: 2011944779

E-book ISBN 978-0-7624-4495-3

9 8 7 6 5 4 3 2 1

Digit on the right indicates the number of this printing

Cover and interior design by Jason Kayser

Typography: Forza, Snoogle, and Tungsten

Running Press Book Publishers

2300 Chestnut Street

Philadelphia, PA 19103-4371

Visit us on the web!

www.runningpress.com

Maybe you've been too busy playing the latest Call of Duty to notice, but concern over video game addiction is gripping our nation. "But I'm no addict!" you might be thinking, though secretly, to yourself, you wonder . . .

Thanks to this book, you'll know for sure.

☐ If you answer, "Yep, that's me!" to ⅓ or less of the following, you're safe. For now. But when that new Call of Duty comes out . . .

☐ If you answer, "Oh, boy—I do that . . ." to half of the following, you're borderline. You're half in the digital world, half in reality. Better part ways with Mario, Master Chief, and Madden, just to be safe.

A 2005 *New York Times* article estimated
that 100,000 Chinese people earned a full-time
income from MMOGs by selling in-game loot
to Western clients for real-world dollars.
Today, industry experts suggest that number is
likely more than half a million.

You tell your uncle, who sucks at Mario Kart,
that he's "wiitarded."

Deciding between groceries and a new wireless gaming headset is a difficult choice.

You used to think video games might be bad for you, so you stopped thinking.

The ratio of gaming consoles to people in your house is greater than 4:1.

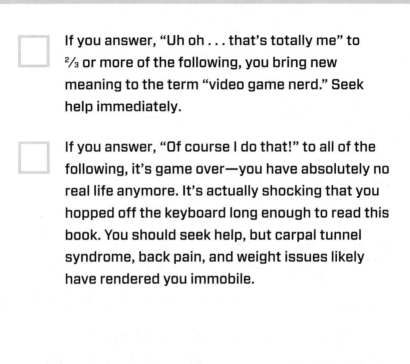

☐ If you answer, "Uh oh . . . that's totally me" to ²/₃ or more of the following, you bring new meaning to the term "video game nerd." Seek help immediately.

☐ If you answer, "Of course I do that!" to all of the following, it's game over—you have absolutely no real life anymore. It's actually shocking that you hopped off the keyboard long enough to read this book. You should seek help, but carpal tunnel syndrome, back pain, and weight issues likely have rendered you immobile.

You consider Rock Star energy drinks, microwavable bean burritos, BBQ potato chips, and Klondike bars a balanced diet.

You buy official video game guide books . . .
and then correct them.

Your personal checks feature Super Mario.

DID YOU KNOW?

**The average social networking gamer
is 42, female, and wouldn't consider herself
a video gamer.**

You remember important dates by their relation to video game releases. ("My wedding? Let's see . . . that was the week before Call of Duty 3 came out.")

* * *

Your top criteria for a spouse?
That they play video games too.

* * *

You went outside once, but the sound quality and graphics just weren't all that good.

Your office dry erase board has more cheat codes than phone numbers.

You have the exact same game on your PlayStation 3, Xbox 360, Wii, computer, and iPhone.

You're more turned on by Lara Croft than Jessica Alba or Megan Fox.

You've worn an adult diaper to get through a gaming session without interruption.

**You've used the phrase "He timed out"
to refer to a real-life death.**

You choose *GamePro* magazine
over *Hustler*.

Watching *Tron* is a near-orgasmic experience.

You buy the soundtracks for your favorite
video games.

You sometimes talk about your characters
in the first person.

You've sent a fan letter to a video game designer.

DID YOU KNOW?

When Google released a free Pac-Man game
on May 21, 2010, it cost U.S. companies
an estimated $120 million in lost productivity
on that day alone!

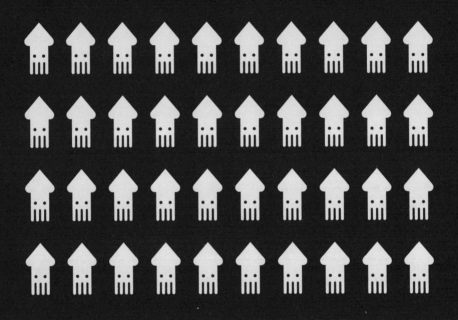

You can't eat calamari without thinking of
the aliens from Space Invaders.

You consider homeschooling the kids so you'll have someone to game with during the week.

You get a game or two in before you get out of bed each morning.

You've used old video game discs as convenient drink coasters.

You're jealous of your character's significant other.

Your résumé describes you as a "level 85 frost mage."

You have more than one handheld video game system in the bathroom.

Your characters have more friends than you do.

You've looked into the legality
of marrying a video game character.

You've participated in a Pac-Man
"play with the screen off" contest . . . and won.

Research indicates 3 billion hours a week are spent playing online video games.

People don't recognize you without a headset on and a controller in your hand.

※ ※ ※

The phrase "just one more level" costs you a dozen sick days each year.

You practice for your Driver's Ed
test by playing Mario Kart, Grand Theft Auto,
and Burnout.

You're convinced that the top three
reasons to have a Facebook account are FarmVille,
Mafia Wars, and Café World.

The power company and the local Best Buy
send you birthday cards.

You've been given more than one
"Body by Nintendo" T-shirt.

You want your first Atari game system to be
buried with you.

Your computer costs far more—and runs more smoothly—than your car.

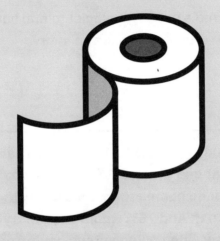

You've looked into retrofitting your gaming chair with a toilet.

You hired a pet psychologist to find out why those birds are so angry.

✳ ✳ ✳

A study by the U.K. newspaper *The Sun* shows that one in three British men would rather play video games than have sex with their partner. And 75% would choose trying out a new video game versus having sex with their partner.

You continually find yourself saying things like: "I'm going to wash the dishes, but first I'll play just a few minutes of Warcraft."

You fire off "You just got pwned!" texts to your friends after each of your gaming victories.

You once explained, "I'm not addicted—I didn't play AT ALL yesterday."

You have a backup Wii system (just in case).

Your Wii backup system has its own backup
(you just never know!).

You feel that any problem can be overcome if you have enough quarters.

You get a Fender Stratocaster for Christmas
and ask where the colored buttons are.

After accidentally putting a needle clean
through your finger, you realize you've entirely lost
all feeling in your hands.

The only names you can think of for your new
puppy are King, Poochy, and Sam.

In arcades across the U.S., you are responsible for hundreds of R-rated leader boards.

```
                    BEST 5

                SCORE        NAME
        1ST     72240        YOU
        2ND     68670        SUK
        3RD     67590        ASS
        4TH     59320        BIG
        5TH     57550        TME
```

Americans spent $2.7 billion on video games in November 2009.

You are one of the nine people who actually watched *The Super Mario Bros. Super Show*.

Video game testing companies are having a bidding war for your services.

You went pro at gaming before you could walk.

You have a "Do Not Disturb—Game
in Progress" tattoo.

You can talk about what happened in a
twenty-minute game for a full hour.

You see food lying on the ground,
and you eat it.

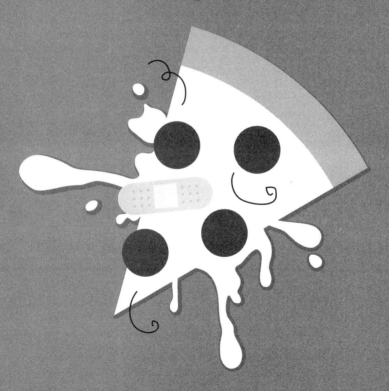

You play Warcraft by this mantra:
"What happens in Azeroth, stays in Azeroth."

✳ ✳ ✳

The phrase "carpal tunnel syndrome"
gives you the willies.

✳ ✳ ✳

Your car sports a "When times get hard,
button mash" bumper sticker.

You expect jewels to appear every time
you mow the lawn.

DID YOU KNOW?

Roughly 114 million American adults—nearly 52% of the entire adult population—regularly play video games, and they have an aggregate income of $4 trillion.

You recall the date, time, and setting of your highest scores for every game you own, but you sometimes forget your kids' birthdays.

You sometimes forget your own birthday.

The only real difference between you and
a pale, basement-dwelling troll? Trolls don't exist.

Your hand-eye coordination is nearly
supernatural.

You paid money to be an extra in *Lara Croft
Tomb Raider: The Cradle of Life*.

Instead of marking your increasing
height on the bedroom wall as you grew up, you
documented your high scores.

You taught yourself Korean and Japanese so
you could play a wider variety of games.

You own a "When I go to the doctor,
I ask how many lives I have left!" baseball cap.

Your ringtone is from Grand Theft Auto.

❄ ❄ ❄

Your DVD collection includes *House of the Dead*,
Mortal Kombat, *Doom*, *Alone in the Dark*,
and *Street Fighter*.

❄ ❄ ❄

The average video game player is 35, male, and
has been playing games for thirteen years.

You believe Justin Bieber is so
popular only because he looks like Chris from
King of Fighters.

✳ ✳ ✳

Instead of counting sheep, you go to sleep
by counting zerglings.

Your high school yearbook includes the goal:
"Save the princess, save the world."

After meeting online game partners
face-to-face, you realize that you like their characters
better than you like them.

You dream about being able to teleport
to the mailbox versus having to walk all the
way there and back.

You frame screenshots.

You expect every plumber to be Italian, wear a jumpsuit, have a mustache, and carry a giant hammer.

After breaking your leg, you crouch
behind a tree and expect to heal in five seconds.

You've stripped down and rebuilt
every video game system you own.
Just because.

You get teary-eyed during the *Max Payne* movie.

According to a May 2009 study in *Psychological Science*, about 8.5% of American youth between 8 and 18 show symptoms of video game addiction.

You've adjusted your sleep pattern to take advantage of your Warcraft server's auction house cycles.

You tried to double jump
in gym class.

You cried when you were told that that
Pokémon weren't real.

You refer to your new car as your "epic mount."

You've mastered playing the PSP
while driving.

When bad things happen in real life,
you reach for the pause button.

You wish there were a higher difficulty level in
Halo than Legendary.

You've got more than one pinup of Princess Peach on your wall.

Your favorite Sunday morning routine is staying in bed, watching reruns of *Adventures of Sonic the Hedgehog*, and playing GameBoy until noon.

Your holy grail is the perfect Pac-Man score: 3,333,360.

**Research shows that 92% of children
and adolescents ages 2-17 play video games.**

You yell, "That's Bryan Fury!" every time you
see Robert Patrick in a film.

You play SIMS just to see what it's like
to date someone.

You dodge traffic on the highway during rush hour to improve your Frogger skills.

You call babies "n00bs."

You've heard the phrase: "If you don't
turn off that damn machine, you're sleeping alone!"

Some people belong to Team Jacob
and some belong to Team Edward, but you
belong to Team Bloodrayne.

Your perfect day is:

1) Wake up

2) Play video games

3) Eat breakfast

4) Play video games

5) Eat lunch

6) Play video games

7) Eat snack

8) Play video games

9) Eat dinner

10) Play video games

11) Eat snack

12) Play video games

13) Go to bed

14) Play video games

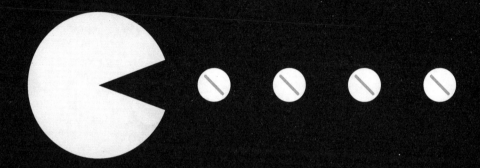

You've actually suffered from "Pac-Man Fever."

You have a kid named Link.

DID YOU KNOW?

A study of 552 Americans by the U.S. Center
for Disease Control found that those who play
video games are more likely to be overweight
and suffer mental health problems.

Your doorbell plays the God of War theme.

A policeman asks for your I.D. and you
give him your Xbox Live username.

Through an energetic e-mail campaign, you're
lobbying Hollywood producers to create
films for Burgertime, Castle Wolfenstein, and
The Oregon Trail.

You learned how to skateboard so you could
do better at the Tony Hawk games.

* * *

When you get angry, you often shout,
"Don't make me go Zelda on you!"

You've camped outside a store for more than 24 hours for a video game release.

You have far more Chuck Norris jokes than
you do friends.

You assume people are lying
when they say there's more music than
what's on Guitar Hero.

Your heroes include Fatal1ty, Leeroy Jenkins,
and Billy L. Mitchell.

You thought the tagline from *The Sixth Sense* was, "I see fragged people."

❋ ❋ ❋

DID YOU KNOW?

A Japanese book, *Brain Pollution*, argues that there's a link between ADHD and children/teens who play first-person shooter video games four or more hours a day.

You're still a member of Club Penguin.

* * *

You blame your parents for bad
parenting because they didn't let you play video
games until you were eight.

* * *

You've had finger calluses almost as
long as you've had fingers.

You can't understand why people don't simply disappear when they die.

You told someone, "Yo momma's so fat, it takes four mages to teleport her!"

You think it's normal to have a machine gun nest in your backyard.

You've been arrested at Pier 1 for smashing open barrels.

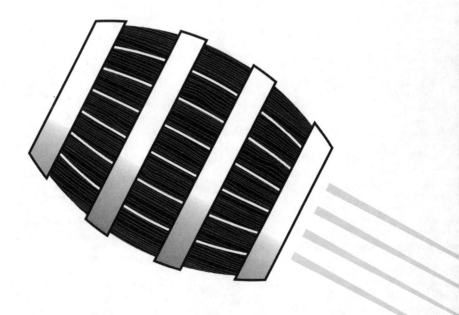

You die a little inside when there's a blackout.

You suffer nightmares over the Video Game
Crash of 1983.

You've had a Wetrix dream.

DID YOU KNOW?

**The video gamer population includes 25 million
adults in the 55+ bracket, 13 million retirees,
and 28 million grandparents.**

Every time you spot a turtle,
you jump on it.

You signed other high school yearbooks with
"All your base are belong to us."

You live by the motto: "Don't fly anything
you're not prepared to lose."

You pity people who can't beat Devil May Cry 3
on Dante Must Die! mode.

When the weatherman announces a flood warning,
you get out your shotgun.

You stuck with TimeSplitters: Future Perfect
until you unlocked all 150 characters.

You know what an ocarina is thanks to Zelda.

You consider it to be a great LAN party if everyone's out of ammo, someone's naked, and the cases of Red Bull are all gone.

* * *

You look into a new video gamer fantasy camp you heard about and find out that for $5,000, people can come and live with you for a week.

**The pizza guy knows to pass you the
box through the window of your gaming room
versus continuing to ring the doorbell.**

> To date, 20% of Facebook gamers have paid
> real-world money for in-game benefits.

You bought a big-screen TV so Sonic can
be life-sized.

You're hooked on Hot Pockets.

You use an IV for long game sessions.

✳   ✳   ✳

You use a catheter, too.

You wonder why Vampire Hunter D looks so much like Red Mage from Final Fantasy.

The words "Game Over" are a challenge you can't ignore.

You gave up beer because it made you too sleepy to keep playing.

You know that Super Mario's original name
was "Mr. Video."

You know that Mario's last name
is "Mario," too.

You dressed up like Faith Connors for Halloween
and haven't taken off the outfit since.

✳ ✳ ✳

**According to one study, one in four kids
acknowledges that their video game
playing can interfere with homework and
academic performance but they haven't done
anything to change their habits.**

The phrase "nerd rage" doesn't upset you.

You've helped Chinese gamers
escape to America so they could play without
governmental restriction.

You use mouthwash instead of a toothbrush
so you can keep your hands free for
the Nintendo DS.

By the time a blockbuster game is
released, you're already sick of playing
your pirated copy of it.

Arguing about whether video game addiction
exists or not is the only thing that gets you to put down
the controller for a moment.

You insist that everyone have an opinion
on which franchise is best: Halo, Call of Duty,
or BioShock.

Hot lava pits, falling blocks, and aliens haunt your dreams.

You feel naked without a controller or keyboard in your hands.

You lie about having ADD symptoms because Ritalin helps you play better.

You refer to being sent out for groceries or gas as a "fetch quest."

You devour your body weight in junk food with each gaming session.

You talked your parents into playing a first-person shooter against you . . . then you didn't hold back like you promised you would.

Loaning out all of your World of Warcraft
materials and not getting them back would be
a serious financial blow.

* * *

You think *The King of Kong: A Fistful of Quarters* is
a better underdog movie than *Rocky*.

* * *

You have dreams from your character's
perspective.

You mastered the art of running from your gaming chair to the bathroom, peeing, then running back . . . all in less than nine seconds.

BLOOD **COFFEE**

The coffee to blood ratio in your system is nearly 1:1.

You're so good at Assassin's Creed that the
C.I.A. has a file on you.

At best, you have a 1 in 4 chance to guess the correct season.

Your favorite web TV show is *The Guild*.

DID YOU KNOW?

A 2007 study by the American Medical Association suggests that more than 5 million American kids (age 8–18) meet the definition of a video game addict.

The cops arrived at your door after the neighbors heard you during a heated PvP match and assumed it was a domestic disturbance.

Over your front door is this plaque:
"Home is where the hearthstone is."

When someone talks about MUD, you don't
think of damp dirt.

You'd rather break both kneecaps
than break a finger.

You discard things versus throw them away.

* * *

You avoid rooms with a lot of people
because there might be lag.

* * *

You suspect the secret to immortality is
"up up down down left right left right B A start."

You marry someone you met on EverQuest.

And you've still never met them
face-to-face.

You modified an
old Nintendo Duck Hunt
zapper pistol
for full auto fire.

Every time you eat a mushroom you expect to grow bigger.

* * *

DID YOU KNOW?

A Hawaii man, Craig Smallwood, sued the makers of Lineage II for gross negligence after playing more than 20,000 hours between 2004 and 2009. U.S. District Judge Alan Kay, who reviewed the claim in 2010, chose not to dismiss it.

YouTube videos of your gaming sessions
have more views than most countries have people.

Your friends might have an intervention
for you if they weren't so busy trying
to top your high scores.

You've never played organized sports, but
you've won the Stanley Cup, the Vince Lombardi
Trophy, the Commissioner's Trophy, and the
Larry O'Brien Championship Trophy.

You own leather driving gloves to go with your wireless racing wheel.

You shout, "Kaboom! Headshot!" over the
headset with each Halo kill.

* * *

You compare all new games and game systems
against the "good old SNES days."

* * *

Your fingers naturally fall onto the WASD
keys on the keyboard.

You argue with the PlayStation 3.

You call home to check on your game systems.

DID YOU KNOW?

> **Roughly 31 million people play FarmVille
> every day.**

You voted for Sauron for president because
he ignores Fog of War, gets +5 attack to all units in any
one region, and has a great production bonus.

Your dog left and it took you three weeks to notice.

You consider playing at Wimbledon after a
good run at Wii Sports.

You actually bought the Call of Duty: Black Ops edition Jeep.

You can't bring yourself to delete games off your hard drive even if you haven't played them in years.

After running out of batteries for the PSP while flying across the U.S., you went into withdrawal so bad they had to land the plane.

You still have games on 5¼" floppies.

You have a video game blog but you're too busy
gaming to post anything.

You pack yourself a bag lunch before you sit
down to play each day.

Sometimes you pretend to have a picnic
by eating in front of a window and playing Ant
Smasher on your iPhone.

DID YOU KNOW?

By the age of 21, the typical American has spent
10,000 hours playing computer games.

Despite not going outside, you have a decent tan thanks to the glow from your monitor.

You're pleased with every bout of insomnia
because it's that much extra time
for gaming.

You regularly have to replace keyboards
because the letters wear out.

Instead of snoring, you game in your sleep.

When asked to "Feed the dog," you fire up
the Nintendogs game versus actually
giving kibble to Fido.

Every new computer virus sends you into a panic.

You will debate anyone, anytime,
anywhere about whether a pirate, ninja, or
cyborg would win in a fight.

You hold funerals for broken gaming equipment.

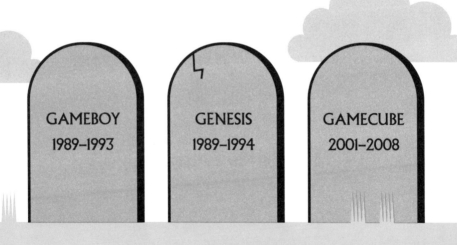

GAMEBOY
1989–1993

GENESIS
1989–1994

GAMECUBE
2001–2008

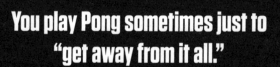

You play Pong sometimes just to "get away from it all."

You have multiple GameFly accounts.

DID YOU KNOW?

After a 15-year-old Swedish boy collapsed and went into convulsions after playing for 24 hours straight, Swedish therapist Sven Rollenhagen called the World of Warcraft "the crack cocaine of the computer gaming world."

You actually own a hedgehog named Sonic.

Seeing a Commodore 64 gives you the
warm fuzzies.

Your idea of justice comes from DC Universe Online.

You use two computers to play online
with yourself.

Your couch has a perfectly formed butt groove.

You have a mortgage with Nintendo.

You paid someone to hack your character's stats to God-like levels.

You tweet about your game achievements as you're playing.

You can't pass a GameStop without a little window-shopping.

You signed a petition to stop Devil May Cry
from migrating to the Xbox 360.

You started the petition to stop Devil May Cry
from migrating to the Xbox 360.

You completed "Through the Fire and Flames" on expert level in Guitar Hero 3 . . . on the first try.

You regularly teabag corpses.

DID YOU KNOW?

More young children know how to play a computer game (58%) than swim (20%) or ride a bike (52%).

One of your life's defining moments occurred
in a video game.

You get stuck on elevators for hours
because you keep pushing all of the buttons.

You logged over 100 days of game time
on World of Warcraft . . . during the first year
you owned the game.

You think that running into a
mirror will teleport you.

You check to see if your cooking skill went
up after you made breakfast.

You've been gaming for two-thirds of your life.

You think the bloody heart "Meg" Easter
egg in Halo is terribly romantic.

DID YOU KNOW?

Each day, school-age children pack almost 8 hours worth of media exposure into 5.5 hours thanks to media multi-tasking.

You take the "Which Video Game Character Am I?" quiz on Facebook and argue over the results.

You have a World of Warcraft VISA card.

You know lots of Intellivision jokes that used to be funny once.

✳ ✳ ✳

You once took out the schoolyard bully thanks to all that training from Mike Tyson in Punch-Out!!

✳ ✳ ✳

Your spouse sends you an in-game message versus shouting for you to come down for dinner.

You spend more real money to buy in-game money from gold farmers than you do anything else.

❄ ❄ ❄

You briefly tried to become a gold farmer but couldn't bring yourself to sell anything that you acquired. You just never know when you might need it!

❄ ❄ ❄

Your entire Christmas list can be covered by a visit to Best Buy.

You have enough empty pizza boxes
to wall off a room.

The villain in *South Park*'s "Make Love, Not Warcraft" episode was based on you.

❄ ❄ ❄

In February 2002, a Louisiana woman sued Nintendo because her son died after suffering seizures allegedly caused by playing his Nintendo 64 for eight hours a day, six days a week.

❄ ❄ ❄

You didn't feel like ripping your hair out when you read, "You are in a maze of twisty passages, all alike."

You know where the phrase
"You have died of dysentery" comes from.

You can play the Super Mario theme
on the piano . . . forwards or backwards.

You think you're qualified to be
president because you scored 38k playing
Civilization IV.

You have more "One time, while I was playing . . ."
anecdotes than you do stories about
your own family.

Your monthly iPhone app bill exceeds your rent.

You still have a Nintendo 64 around so
you can go "old school" and play GoldenEye 007,
Perfect Dark, and Ogre Battle 64.

You refuse to watch the Academy Awards after *Prince of Persia* didn't make the short list for Best Picture.

While others might have pondered over "Ginger or Mary Ann," you've spent hours debating SoulCalibur's Ivy or Sophitia.

You believe that spending a year of your life getting every Horde achievement in World of Warcraft is a fair trade-off.

In a two-year study of more than 3,000 school children in Singapore, researchers found nearly 1 in 10 were video game addicts.

You've earned the "Seriously 3.0" achievement on Gears of War. Twice.

You can tell an Xbox and Xbox 360 game
apart from a half-mile away.

You have more broken keyboards, mice, joysticks,
and controllers than you do working ones.

You know the difference between a voulge,
a glaive, and a Lochaber axe.

You were acquitted for murdering your roommate
after he threw out your Atari 2600.

Powering off a game before it's over is a hanging
offense in your home.

You've crossed out and corrected anything
on this list.

You've thought of ten or twelve more
additions to this list.

You thought you'd died and gone to heaven
when you saw this ad: "Discover how to earn a GREAT
income playing video games without having
to get an expensive college degree!"

You were acquitted for murdering your roommate after he threw out your Atari 2600.

Powering off a game before it's over is a hanging offense in your home.

You've crossed out and corrected anything
on this list.

You've thought of ten or twelve more
additions to this list.

You thought you'd died and gone to heaven
when you saw this ad: "Discover how to earn a GREAT
income playing video games without having
to get an expensive college degree!"

You have a tattoo that reads, "It's time to split!"

* * *

South Park tackled the issue of video game addiction in their Emmy-winning season 10 episode, "Make Love, Not Warcraft."

* * *

You legally changed your name to "Master Chief."

GAME OVER